Tabligh Movement

Maulana Wahiduddin Khan

THE ISLAMIC CENTRE
New Delhi

Translated by Farida Khanam

Urdu version: *Tablighi Tahreek*

First published 1986
Reprinted 1992, 1994, 1996, 1997, 1999, 2003

Goodword Books Pvt. Ltd.
1, Nizamuddin West Market
New Delhi 110 013
Tel. 2435 5454, 2435 6666, 2435 5729
Fax 2435 7333, 2435 7980
e-mail: info@goodwordbooks.com
www.goodwordbooks.com

Contents

1

MAULANA ILYAS

It was a cold day in winter. The year 1966. I alighted from a train at a station on the North Eastern Railway. On my way back home, I was struck by something rather remarkable in the appearance of a group of pedestrians who were hurrying to cross the street. Dressed in coarse, simple clothes, with bags and beddings on their shoulders, they somehow had a religious aura about them as they pressed onwards. In those now far-off days they looked like creatures from another world, but nowadays they have become such a familiar sight that they hardly need description.

Innumerable people of this kind travelling in caravans, have opted for the hard way to serve the cause of God. Many such groups, by turns, are constantly on the move. This great movement generally known as Tablighi Jama'at, has inspired in people a new fervour, a new zeal to serve the divine cause. Its founder surprisingly was a slight, short-statured individual, rather unimpressive in personality. There were times when he found it difficult to express himself because of his bad stammer due to the impediment in his speech. It was this extraordinary figure, known as Maulana Ilyas, who founded the Tablighi Jama'at, which was to inspire in thousands of people a religious zeal which had been unknown for centuries. Although frail to the point of physical weakness, he possessed great inner strength which provided solutions to every problem he was confronted with. His indomitable will and staunchness of purpose in guiding people along the right path lead him to exert himself in a manner which many a physically stronger person would have found arduous.

Early Circumstances

If one climbed a high building in Delhi at the turn of the 19th century, one could see a few buildings scattered here and there in the vicinity of sprawling jungles. This was the place famous for the shrine of Nizamuddin Aulia, which has given its name to the place. Maulana Mohd Ismail, a religious scholar, who died in 1898, lived there. In his eagerness to help the people, he had taken to seeking out labourers in that forsaken place, offering them his help, and fetching water for them to drink. Then he would say a prayer of thanks that God had granted him the opportunity to serve His servants.

It was this saintly person who was the father of Maulana Ilyas. This family traced its descent to the Valiullahi family, who had been chosen by God to rectify the distorted picture of Islam which had resulted from the Taimur family's wrong attitude towards religion. He was born into a family where there was no need to have recourse to make-believe stories for inspiration, as there had been a whole series of such devoted people in his family whose true stories of sacrifice in the path of God very well served the purpose. Even the women would tell their babies the stories of their forefathers who had, at all costs, dedicated themselves to the divine path. Religion was practised to the letter. The mothers in this family naturally did not wish material success for their children. On seeing extraordinary abilities in them, they did not say, like common people, "This child will be rich and great." They said rather, "This child reminds me of the companions of the prophet. We wish he could follow the same path." It was in such an atmosphere that the Maulana grew up.

His parents owned a bookshop which was managed by his elder brother, Maulana Yahya. Maulana Ilyas, being too weak for physical exertion, could not undertake to help his elder brother in his work. Instead, he devoted his time and attention to religious studies, while his elder brother worked hard to run the bookshop. One day the manager suggested to him that Maulana Ilyas should also be engaged in the work. Maulana Yahya, was quite disconcerted at his remark, and replied, "The prophet has said, 'You owe your provision to the weaker members of your family.' I believe that it is owing to this child that I am provided for." He further admonished him not to say such things to him in future, In this atmosphere of absolute purity of thought, word and deed, it was natural that his emotions and feelings should be cast in the same mould. One of the Maulana's classfellows has narrated an incident which took place when he was a student. "One day," he said, "The Maulana brought a stick, and holding it in his hand, he said, "Come, my dear Riyazul Islam, let us declare holy war on those who do not say their prayers."

After completing his school education, he went on to higher studies. Soon he was offered the post of teacher at the Mazahirul Islam religious school at Saharanpur. But before long, new opportunities opened out before him, and his training period commenced. His father had set up a small religious school in Basti Hazrat Nizamuddin to impart free education to poor students. After the death of his father, the elder brother had taken charge of it. When, on this sad occasion, he came home to offer his condolence the people who were running the school insisted on his staying there and taking up his father's cause. He acceded to their request.

Now there began a new phase in his life. It was at this place that he first came into contact with the Mewatis. Distressed by their religious and spiritual poverty, he set himself to reform their condition through religious education. The initial stimulus for his work thus came from Mewati Muslims. Gaining momentum gradually, the work of bringing people closer to the path of God, spread far and wide.

Mewat is a region situated to the south of Delhi, its inhabitants being known as Meo. These people could be described as semi-tribal, somewhat like the ancient Arab bedouins. These uncouth and illiterate people had converted to Islam on a mass scale as a result of the efforts of the well-known sufi Hazrat Nizamuddin Aulia and his descendants. But in practical life they were very far from Islam. There was nothing Islamic about them apart from the title of Muslims that they bore. They kept their Hindu names, like Nahar Singh and Bhup Singh; they left a lock of hair on the top of the shaven head as Hindus do; they worshipped idols, celeberated all the Hindu festivals and made sacrifices to the pre-Islamic gods and goddesses. Also on the occasion of Shab-e-Barat they hoisted the flag of Sayyed Salar Ghazi, a Muslim saint, who had been adopted by them as an object of idolatory. They could not even recite the creed of the Muslims. So unfamiliar even was the sight of prayer, let alone the saying of it, that if by chance they came across someone praying, they gathered to enjoy the spectacle, assuming that the person must either be mad or suffering from some ailment due to which he was kneeling and prostrating himself again and again. Like tribal peoples they were scantily-clad, and spent most of their time in robbing, looting and other such base occupations. Small trifling matters led to prolonged wars such as the pre-Islamic Arab Bedouins had engaged in. They were a brave and sturdy people, but their lack of education and training had come in the way of their advancing beyond the tribal way of life. Major Piolet, the Bandobast officer of Alwar, at the end of the 19th century, writes:

> "Meo are half-Hindus in their habits and customs."

They had posed a serious threat to the Muslim rule in the initial Sultanate period, looting and plundering the city at night. For fear of their attacks, the gates of the capital were closed at dusk. No one dared to go out after dark. Sultan Ghyasuddin Balban in the year 1266 dispatched an expedition against them in which a great number of them were put to the sword, but they were never fully subdued. Even as late as the period of the British Raj, the government was only partially successful in crushing them and establishing peace in the area.

In 1921 new problems arose when Arya preachers resolved to reconvert the Indian Muslims to their ancestral religion. Thanks to the religious and cultural poverty of the Meos, the large-scale activities of the Aryan missionaries met with great success. The solution to this problem was to impart to them religious education so that they did not yield to any malign influence.

Maulana Ilyas, like his father and brother visited Mewat from time to time. Basti Hazrat Nizamuddin being not far from there. Some Mewati students were already studying there and many other Mewatis had came to hold the family of Maulana Ilyas in great reverence because of their devotion and struggle to guide them along the right path. But there was still much to do, and the Maulana, greatly moved by their plight, felt a strong urge to improve their condition. His first idea was to set up and run schools in this area of Mewat on the pattern set by his family, so that the local children could have easy access to education.

When it came to convincing the Mewatis that they should send their children to school, they were tough nuts to crack. How could they spare their children for school? This, for them amounted to a sheer waste of time. The children regularly helped their parents in ploughing, grazing the cattle and other such activities. So the idea of supporting their children without any return from them had no appeal. But the Maulana was the last man to accept defeat. he did not weaken in his resolve, but rather intensified his campaign, sometimes approaching them personally, and sometimes entering their congregations to plead his case. He would tell them, "If only you would spare your children, I would take the responsibility for all their expenses at the school." They ultimately surrendered before his indomitable will, and he succeeded in establishing a number of schools where, besides the teaching of the Quran, elementary religious education was also imparted. Work on this pattern continued until another incident occurred which changed the course of his activities. On a visit to Mewat, the Maulana was introduced to a young man who had just completed his education in one of his schools. Much to his astonishment, he saw no traces of

Islam in his clean-shaven appearance. He was quick to relaize his failure. His aim had not been fulfilled. He had been aware of this problem to some extent before, but now it had become plain for all to see. The schools did serve a purpose, but to the Maulana's eyes, only a secondary one; that is, it had considerably enhanced his own image and, as he himself was now held in reverence, he was in a better position to bring pressure to bear upon them when it came to solving their disputes; there was no doubt that he was extremely successful in this regard. The Mewatis said, "Though a mere skeleton, when he takes up any issue, he can work wonders. He can solve complicated problems in a matter of minutes. Even the most stubborn of us surrender ourselves before him."

But this was not the main issue. What the Maulana was primarily concerned with was the awakening in them of the religious spirit. Their religious inertia was so deep-rooted that even school courses could not help them to slough it off. This failure of the schools greatly distressed him, and he gave the question much thought. At last **he** arrived at the conclusion that the real inadequacy lay in the present method of working: the attempt to educate them in their own atmosphere and in the scene of their own activities. In such surroundings the best efforts on the part of the teachers were in vain. As soon as the young people left the school they mingled with company of their own sort, which nullified the school influence altogether. The only solution to this problem, as the Maulana saw it, lay in separating them from their milieu, and it was decided that they should be withdrawn from it in group for a period of time, and gathered together in mosques or religious institutions away from bad spheres of influence. Thus detached from their worldly and material atmosphere, they would be imparted education by counsel and guidance in the company of religious people. This formula proved the right one. Engaging them in religious activities round the clock for some length of time made them into new human beings. Once the trial proved effective, this pattern was to be followed in future.

The attempt proved to be harder than the previous one. The Mewatis, loath to spare their children even for part-time study in local schools, could not easily be persuaded to let their children leave home altogether. But the Maulana's sincerity of intention, perseverance, and prayers came to his rescue once again. Gradually a new consciousness was awakened in them, and his efforts were finally rewarded. Here are two of the many incidents in his career which will convey the hardship that he experienced in taming this unyielding nation.

Once, during one of his preaching missions, Maulana Ilyas put his hand lovingly on the shoulders of a Mewati, only to have him fly into a rage and shout at him. "If you ever touch me with your hand again, I'll give you a good beating." The cool and calm Maulana immediately bent to his feet saying, "You did not forbid me to touch your feet, did you?"

Similarly, once, when he was impressing upon a Mewati the importance of leading a religious life, the Mewati, instead of paying heed to the message, dealt him a hard blow. The Maulana was so frail physically that he collapsed. When he regained consciousness, he got up and caught hold of his assailant's shirt. "You have done your job," he said, now listen to me!" Here was someone who, instead of taking revenge, asked only the favour of being listened to with patience. The Mewati was touched. He fell at his feet and begged his forgiveness saying, that if he were not to be forgiven, he should be eternally condemned.

This latter incident, besides showing his sincerity and eagerness, also shows how his concern for their welfare had turned to anguish. He was willing to go to any lengths for the sake of impressing upon them the eternal realities.

Such involvement could not fail to reap dividends: large numbers of people were brought into his fold from various parts of the country to spread the message he entrusted them with. Staying day and night in a religious and spiritual atmosphere indeed worked wonders for them for when those people returned home after having under-gone the training, they were changed people. Far from fal-

11

ling under the bad influence of their surroundings, they set out to be a good influence on their environment. The Maulana had found the solution to his problem.

The whole of Mewat was transformed. Great spiritual excitement and enthusiasm could be seen among the people at large. Where previously, mosques had been few and far between, now mosques and religious schools came up in every settlement. Not only had they increased in number and size, but the local people had also come to appreciate their activities. They changed their way of dressing and grew beards, shaking off one by one almost all the pre-Islamic customs that they had retained after their conversion. Lending or borrowing on interest as well as robbing, looting, and dacoities decreased considerably. Liquor consumption came to an end. Almost every child became punctual at his prayers. Their dealings, behaviour and living standards were all influenced as a result of this religious awakening. Not only did they reform themselves but they were also inspired to spread the true message of God to those who were as ignorant as they had been before. Their simple, sincere stories of devotion made it seem as if history were repeating itself, as if the newly converted Bedouins, inspired with new found zeal were reborn and roaming across the desert, their only desire being to spread the message far and wide.

In September 1929, an elderly, religious person visited the area to observe personally the much talked-of religious fervour. He found on his way a group of simple Mewati villagers who were going out on a religious expedition. He motioned to one of them to stop and asked him, "What is all this movement for?" The Mewati replied, There was a time when we were neither aware of our God nor of our messenger. May God now bless the Maulvi who showed us the right path. Our only wish is now to convey this great blessing to others." The truth expressed in such simple words, so succinctly, reminded one of a speech made by Jafar, a compantion of the Prophet, before Najjashi, the Christian king of Habash.

The Sincere Devotion

The success of a mission does not rest only on its being true, but also on the sincerity and zeal of the people involved. Maulana Ilyas burned with such zeal and was willing to face all difficulties and hardships that came his way. It is the initiative of such a person which inevitably carries him through to a successful conclusion.

Once a colleague of the Maulana visited his house to offer his condolence, when the Maulana had passed away. He sent a message to his wife, asking her to tell him something about the Maulana. This is what she replied.

"When I was married to him, I came to stay with him. I found that the Maulana hardly slept at nights. I could hear him moaning and groaning in bed. One day I asked him what it was that was disturbing his sleep. He sighed and replied, 'Would that you knew of my suffering and shared my agony, I would not be alone then. There would be two of us to keep awake at nights."

The Maulana's stammering, and, the complexities of traditional religious style made it difficult for him to express himself. But, thanks to his total involvement, his whole body seemed to convey the message. He groaned, and restless as a fish out of water, he would say repeatedly: "I am unable to do anything, my God. I am too weak." The people could not help but feel pity for him. His unbounded will, however, made him overcome all obstacles. He even outdid all his companions who were more physically fitted for the job. He could walk across rough, uneven stretches of Mewat for as far as 25 miles at a time without taking any food and water. His hectic life left him no time to look after himself. Many a time he left Nizamuddin on a Friday after lunch and had his second meal only after returning home on a Sunday. Keeping awake at nights, climbing mountains, making his way through the hot, dry plains of Mewat, and alternately facing waves had almost become a routine with him. When he found that his colleages were almost dropping with exhaustion from such a busy schedule, he observed: "God is but beyond the mountain of struggle: whoever wants to see Him can find Him there."

When someone enquired after his health, he wrote back: "How does health matter? One can be said to be well if one is able to properly perform the task for which one was born."

Once some relatives from Kandhla, his hometown, visited him to enquire after his health. On hearing about it, he said, "You have traversed such a long distance to learn about one who is born to die, whereas the religion of the Prophet Muhammad, which is eternal, is being neglected, and you show no concern for it."

When he was seriously ill, the doctors advised him refrain from speaking, but he said, "I prefer to die while exhorting people to the path of the Lord, than to take rest for the recovery of my own health."

As his health deteriorated, he received repeated inquiries about it. Replying to one of his friends, he writes:

"I have no pain except that of preaching."

It greatly distressed him to learn that only the less educated have surrendered themselves to his fold. On his death-bed, he writes with great pain:

"Would that the religious scholars were to take up
the cause before I passed away."

Once while saying his prayers in the train, his colleagues stopped others from passing in front of him. When he had finished his prayers, he showed his resentment and said, "You had better set up a Sutrah*. This was because of his great consideration for others.

On one journey to Kandhla he bought a third class ticket but, having failed to find a seat in a third class compartment, he got into a second class compartment along with his colleagues. He could pay the extra amount

---

*Something put up before one engaged in prayer to prevent others from intruding upon the worshippers' devotions. It may be a stick, or anything a cubit in height and an inch in thickness.

when the ticket collector arrived, he said. But the ticket collector created difficulties when he saw the tickets. The Maulana was momentarily put out and scolded him. When the Ticket Collector left after renewing the tickets, one of his colleagues, Maulana Inamul Hasan, said to him that the man had had the right to object. The Maulana was quick to admit his mistake and as soon as the train stopped at the next station, he went up to him and apologized.

His attachment to God was such that prayers were not so much a matter of obligation to him as a source of great enjoyment and solace. In the course of rough journeys where hills had to be crossed, his colleagues were usually exhausted by the time they reached the top of the hill and prefered to take rest. But not the Maulana. He would stand up on the top of hills in prayer for hours.

When he died, his body had been given a bath, and was being perfumed, when one of his close colleagues said: "Perfume his forehead well, it used to stay in prostration for hours."

His heart-felt prayers, sacrifices, his attachment to God gave such force and effect to his mission that today it makes people wonder at the astonishing results achieved, as they find it hard to explain this phenomenal success in material terms.

Here is a short extract from one of his letters which shows the degree of his involvement:

> "The results are in proportion to one's struggle. The more one humbles oneself before the Lord, and bears the hardship in this path; the more one is entitled to divine succour."

These words give an accurate picture of the Maulana himself. In actual fact, his self-abnegation in God's path was total, and this gave peculiar vision and penetration to his words. When one has fully devoted oneself to one's cause, one's personality takes on such depth that it penetrates the very hearts of the listener.

Here are some more excerpts from his speeches to this effect.

"This is the most important task; a pearl among pebbles. Sacrifice your lives for this cause. The more you forsake materially the more you gain spiritually."

Once as some guests were leaving, the Maulana said to them, "You came and stayed just as guests. Remember, the cause of God involves forsaking even the barest necessities of life like food and water. Sweat in this path and be ready to shed your blood."

In one of his letters to Issa, a friend of his, he expresses regret at those who refrained from becoming involved in this mission.

"Issa, think, how all members of a family engage themselves in this ephemeral world, whereas not even one of them is willing to spare a little of his time for God. Does this not imply holding this world superior to the next world?"

Once a Tabligh gathering was held in Lucknow. After the meeting, a group of people began to exhort the audience to offer to go to Kanpur for the sake of the mission. Despite repeated exhortations, not a single person responded to the call. The Maulana was pained to see this indifference. One of the participants, Haji Wali Mohammad, was suffering from piles and obviously was too weak to travel. The Maulana asked him why he lagged behind. He told him that he was almost dying. The Maulana said, "When you are dying already you had better die in Kanpur."

These incidents reveal only partially the degree of his involvement, because, when an incident is reported, the personality of the speaker, the emotions and feelings attached to words are missing. The sincere feelings, the inner conviction, the impassioned and heartfelt longing to make the listeners understand the message — not all of this can be captured in writing.

Once someone came to see the Maulana after attending the congregation. The Maulana asked him, "Didn't you feel sorry for the pathetic abyss we have fallen into?" He replied "Since I have witnessed for myself the ignorance of our community, I'm ashamed of our very existence."

It was as a result of such dedication to the cause that in the first major congregation in Mewat in November 1941, about 25,000 people attended it. A large number of them came walking all the way from as far as fifty miles. Their pitiful lack of education can be judged from the response the Maulana received when he urged one of the Mewatis to work for Tabligh. "Tablid? What is Tablid?" rejoined the Mewati, unable even to pronounce the word. Yet these very people, ignorant of even the term, had been converted as if by magic, into great missionaries, the like of whom the country had never known.

Motivated by an overpowering urge to salvation in the next life; a longing that God should forgive them when they came before Him, they set out to conquer the hearts of the people. When Islam penetrates into the depth of one's consciousness, one becomes concerned with one thing alone: how to earn God's favour and forgiveness. One immediately seeks to mould one's faith, ideas, character and actions on this and all one does in life is in accordance with one's overriding concern to avoid displeasing God. It is on the hereafter that one focusses all one's attention. One calls others to Islam, making sure that one is first a good Muslim oneself. These enthusiastic preachers, roaming across the country, reminded one of the materially resourceless Arab Bedouins, who, inspired by the spiritual wealth of Islam, were to be seen on the move everywhere in order to propagate the truth.

Absolute Trust in Divine Succour

What was it, in the main, that the Maulana gave his followers which completely transformed their lives? what he did was impress upon the people the fact that this world did not spring up by itself, but was created by one God, who continues to watch over it that all men were His servants, responsible to Him for their actions, that death was not the end of man's life; rather it was the beginning of another, permanent world, where the good would enjoy the bliss of paradise and the wicked would be cast into raging hell.

The Maulana impressed upon the people that believing personally was not all that was required of one; one was also entrusted with conveying the word of God to others. All obstacles in the path would be overcome with God's help. Here is an incident which shows how convinced his followers were of the help of God.

Once a Mewati, asked to narrate some event during his preaching career, said "the Maulana once despatched a Jama'at (group) consisting of three men, to Moradabad, I being one of them. On reaching the city he went to a mosque and stayed there. After the Maghrib (evening) prayer, we made an announcement that people should stay for a while after the prayer so that we could discuss some religious issues. But, much to our astonishment, not a single person stayed after the prayer. We waited for the next day. At the same point we made a similar announcement, but to no avail. Once again all the worshippers got up and left without showing any interest. This incident reminded us of the last thing that the Maulana had done. He made us promise that in times of any difficulty we would go away from human settlement to some lonely place and turn to God in solitude. So we stayed that night in the mosque, and as soon as the day broke, all three of us went out of the settlement to pray. We prayed the whole day and returned in the evening to the same mosque. After the Maghrib prayer, the same message was announced. At this point the Mewati paused, as if he was going to unravel some mystery. A mystery it was indeed. He went on, "They all seemed rooted to the spot. Not a single soul stood up to leave. My friends, this is the way our work shall continue, with the help of God."

Here was the evidence that prayer was the power that could shake the world and move mountains. It armed the resourceless and gave them courage to face all obstacles in their path. It was a blessing that made the dumb speak, the blind see and the lame walk; in short, a key to all locked doors.

The history of Tabligh abounds in experience which have endowed its members with such mental and physical powers as enable them to surmount all difficulties. They do not stop short when it comes to taking initiatives, however adverse the circumstances may be. To them prayer is as dependable as anything can be. It is like the magic wand of Moses.

Be it an individual or a community, there is always the need for external support, to give the stability, courage and confidence necessary for survival. In search of such a prop, people tend to look up to some visible material object. Their worldly mentality leads them to think only in terms of worldly sureties and guarantees. Naturally, those who do not own worldly resources are considered ill-fitted to live in this world. But the Tabligh concept of prayer acquaints man with a treasure that has nothing to do with worldly resources. It lays claims only on one's heart which no one can take away from one. When man surrenders his heart to God in total submission, the whole universe capitulates before him.

A concept which bestows upon man such huge reserves of strength; which arms a resourcesless person, surpasses all limitations. Tabligh workers have encountered innumerable miraculous events in their service to God's cause, which is a proof that God has granted them access to this great source. God's blessing will fully mainfest themselves when a whole community is willing to surrender before the will of God. If a whole nation followed this faith, the Maulana had no doubt that God's succour would be ours in its consummate form. It is then that oceans and jungles surrender themselves; the nations capitulate before them. All is possible provided we can tap the source of this moral strength which God will give us if we surrender to Him our hearts and our minds.

It would be pertinent to quote some excerpts from the Quran regarding the forms taken by divine succour. One is mentioned in the Quran in terms of the good life and another in terms of entrusting man with power on earth:

"We shall reward the steadfast according to their noblest deeds. Be they men or women, those that embrace the faith and do what is right We will surely grant a happy life; We shall reward them according to their noblest actions" (16:97).

"Allah has promised those of you who believe and do good works to make them masters in the land as He had made their ancestors before them, to strengthen the Faith He chose for them, and to change their fear to safety. Let them worship Me and serve no other gods besides Me. Wicked indeed are they who after this deny Me" (24.55).

'Good life' here has different aspects: lawful earning; contentment; peace of mind; love of God; enjoyment in worship; success in this life as well as in the next: all of which go to make up a successful life.

The seond form of the blessing descends on a society which has withstood the test by purifying itself. When a considerable number of such good souls comes into being, God's blessing at times takes the form of power on earth, because God wants the religion He has chosen for His servants to be established on earth. The power shall not, however, be inherited like that of kings and emperors, but like that of the descendants of the Prophet, the humble servants of God. They will be granted power so that they can proclaim the divine will on earth and overcoming every obstacle on the path, bring stability to the true religion. Then Muslims will no longer cower before nonbelievers, for they will not fear them; they will not care for any mortal's pleasure or displeasure. Peace will consequently prevail over the world and God's servants will worship Him in peace. They will surrender their wills to Him alone, fearing no one but Him. These blessings that descend upon individuals and on society are in no way an acquisition, but a gift from God. The common ground for deserving such blessings for both the individual and society are faith, good deeds, and being able to prove ourselves worthy of receiving such blessing. Then God, the Omnipotent, who is in control of all events, creates conditions and circumstances to facilitate our discovery of truth. It is through His help that we arrive at the essence of religion.

Thus when a group of individuals fully submits to God and does good deeds, God's blessing embrace the whole of society. As a consequence our activities are brought to fruition and our initiatives yield positive results.

The belief in this concept serves a double function. On the one hand, it strengthens the heart of the preacher; on the other, it brings the hope and conviction that God will melt the hearts of the congregation so that they become receptive to the message.

To Maulana Ilyas, this concept of blessing provided the greatest weapon to the preachers. It gave a preacher the force and inner conviction to face all hardship. He would never yield to pressure, whatever the circumstances, and there would be no challenge which he would not feel well equipped to meet — such would be the resoluteness of his character.

An Appeal to the Heart

Late one evening in October 1930, the renowned poet, Dr. Mohammad Iqbal, received a visitor, who was also a litterateur, at his residence in Lahore. Reclining in his armchair, he was conversing with him on a variety of topics which seemed of great importance and immediacy when he suddenly sat up straight and said to his guest, "why don't you write a book?" His guest was somewhat startled but naturally wanted to know what the subject should be. Dr. Iqbal then launched with great enthusiasm on an explanation of the project which had taken shape in his mind. "Hundreds and thousands of Indians from the villages and outskirts of the towns of India have converted to Islam on their own. If you meet them and inquire about the reasons for their self-conversion, they will reveal strange reasons that appeal to the heart. If all that were to be compiled in book form, it would be of tremendous help to the missionaries." "Don't we already possess enough proofs of the truth of Islam?" the visitor asked "Yes, we do have ample evidence," replied Dr Iqbal, "but contact with the new-converts will unearth such strange, amazing proofs of the veracity of Islam as have hitherto been unknown. This is sure to prove a great asset to the propagation of Islam.

To me, there is a great difference between heart and mind. The mind often discards the most powerful of arguments. On the contrary, the heart is often won over by less forceful arguments, and, to such an extent, that one's whole way of life is transformed altogether in a matter of minutes. The matter of conversion has always related more to the heart than to the mind. What a preacher must learn to aim at is the heart, that is what will serve his purpose best. Many such revolutions in the lives of polytheists and non-believers have been recorded in the history of Islam.

"Normally, thanks to one's traditions and upbringing, one stands as firm as a rock, clinging to this set of traditions or to a religion. For this there is no dearth of arguments appealing to the mind. Yet, all of a sudden, the heart leaps at a new idea, and within seconds, one's whole life is transformed. If a large number of incidents of this type were compiled in book form, I am sure it would not only prove a great asset to our preachers, but would be a kind of cornucopia to the average reader whose religious inclination need circumstantial support."

Perhaps one would be right in saying that Maulana Ilyas' mission, as far as working among poorly educated Muslims is concerned, is the realization of Iqbal's dream. Throughout his life, the Maulana adopted the way through the heart, which worked wonders. There are innumerable examples of this kind. We mention here one of them, showing how he once won the heart of an unruly and stubborn student, who was notorious for his wrongdoing and refusal to submit to school discipline.

This student had once been appointed to collect funds for the school, and thanks to his ingenuity, had managed to collect a donation of Rs. 20,000. But he never handed it over. To the horror of the school authorities, they received instead bundles of works of fiction to the value of the whole amount. Without even opening the bundles, the school sold the books by the kilo. Another misdemeanour occurred when a group of students from an Arabic school in which this boy was also studying, was coming to see the Maulana. His classmates insisted on his accompanying them, and finally, he was persuaded to come to Basti Nizamuddin. But, at night, when everyone had gone to bed, he quietly slipped out, along with some other students, to go to a cinema show in the city. (As Nizamuddin was situated on the outskirts, there were no cinemas there.) When the show was over, they failed to find a conveyance, and had to pass the night in the city.

The Maulana, in the habit of holding a congregation after the morning prayer, came to the pulpit to address the people. He asked the school boys to come nearer, and all of the students did so except two who seemed to be missing from the congregation. The Maulana, assuming that these two could not be very far away, decided to wait for them, and start the sermon when they had arrived. But it took a long time for them to arrive, which in itself seemed very suspicious, and it was soon revealed that they had left the night before for a cinema show.

The manager of the school to which the students belonged was also present at the centre. He was distressed at their bad behaviour. He as well as other authorities, had done their best to reform him, but to no avail. Now the boy had come to be considered incorrigible, as he had resisted all well-meaning efforts to improve him. Now his expulsion from the school was brought under consideration. After the incident, at Nizamuddin, the Manager wrote to the headmaster to order his explusion immediately.

In the meanwhile, his schoolmates were also ashamed. They then hit upon the idea of bringing the matter to the Maulana's notice. One of them, therefore, met him in private and told him the whole story. The Maulana asked them not to get upset and to pray to God to help them.

After the evening prayer, the Maulana asked for pen and paper and sent for the manager of the school. When he arrived, the Maulana told him to write a letter to the headmaster on his behalf. The Maulana himself dictated the letter to him. It read as follows:

"Some students from your school came to our Centre. I am happy at their performance. They have benefited from the religious gatherings at the centre. My prayers are with them. I would request you to honour and welcome them."

Then the Manager was asked to endorse the report. He had no choice but to do as he was bidden. The Maulana saw to it that the letter was posted.

This event brought astonishing results. A student who had been considered totally incorrigible had been transformed into the most sincere and most serious of young men. Later on, he chose to become a volunteer of the Tabligh mission. When asked the reason for his complete transformation, he would simply say, "Maulana Ilyas has captured me." At a point where training and education had failed, prayer had triumphed.

The career of Maulana Ilyas in particular, and the Tabligh mission in general , is full of such instances. The power of prayer, love, character and sympathy has, astonishingly, conquered innumerable hearts. The answering of prayer gives great inspiration to the people associated with the mission. Simplicity, perceptiveness, natural arguments and a realistic approach cannot but fail to move any audience. The Tabligh preachers, so to speak, follow the path of the heart as opposed to that of the mind. This is their greatest asset.

Programme

The Maulana's plan had six important aims. They were:-

1. To implant the significance of Kalimah (The creed of the Muslims): there is no deity but God; Muhammad is His Apostle;
2. To observe prayer as is proper;
3. To acquire religious knowledge;
4. To give due respect to Muslims;
5. to spare time, that is, to withdraw from one's worldly engagements and go forth in missionary groups;
6. To purify one's intentions and to remain sincere and self-appraising.

These six points can be condensed into three:

The Kalimah Tauhid, prayer and sparing time for good

works. The other three are, in actual fact, offshoots of the main tenets. When they are adopted whole-heartedly all other things follow in consequence.

There are many ways of explaining this preaching mission. The Maulana, however, preferred to allude to this programme in terms of the revival of the prophetic way, and would explain it accordingly. This is, no doubt, the most appropriate definition of his work. Considering that there are people who attach importance to things only when they are described in the modern terminologies of psychology, philosophy and science and so on, this programme can likewise be described in any language they can understand, or which has a special significance for them. His message gives prime importance to the Kalimah: to believe in the reality that there is no deity but God, that He alone is the Creator and Nourisher of the universe, and that the truth had been made manifest through his messenger, the Prophet Mohammad (on whom be peace). When one recites these words: there is no deity but God and the Prophet Mohammad is His messenger, it amounts to expressing one's inner feelings of conviction of th truth of these words. It also proclaims one's determination to follow a path based on the firm conviction that God is the only real existence, centre of all our complete trust. This proclamation is an expression of an all-pervasive feeling within one of having at last found the true way of life and also the source from which the truth emanates — the only source whose guidance is worthy of trust.

Trust and conviction are, in fact, the source of all revolution, be it religious or secular. A history of revolution tells us that it was the courage of conviction—right or wrong—in certain souls, which has made history. The revolution of France: the victory of Communism and the freedom movements in various countries were all, in fact, based on such conviction as stimulated them to action. Initially none of these movements had possessed either huge resources of armaments or enormous wealth. They were unable even to conceive fully of what shape their activities were going to take in future; how their theories were going to be put into practice. The only thing that spurred them on to make unflagging efforts was a concept which had preoccupied their thoughts. It was the discovery of some political, economic or nationalistic truths that inspired them to such a degree that they concentrated all their potentialities and energies on making it known to people. For this, they accepted the challenge—however harsh it was, of external opposition and engaged themselves in a fervent struggle; such an effort is inevitably seen through to its conclusion. The only possible result of such initiatives is success.

Yet they were people who had found only a partial truth, wrongly considering it to be the whole truth. One can then imagine what the strength of such a conviction would be like when based on truth in the real sense of the word. When such truths are firmly implanted in one's heart and mind, like a divine fervour, one can gauge what enormous benefits can result. Where other movements have succeeded in influencing only some parts of the world, or only a limited number of people, the true faith has the potential to move all mankind. Who can check the tide of a movement launched by people who have put their total trust in God? When human concepts can bring about revolution, what greater revolution can be brought about through divine concepts!

The Kalimah is thus the essence of religion — the greatest power on earth. The movement can, therefore, be appropriately called a Kalimah movement. But one should not forget that any movement, secular or religious, is essentially a movement of words — be they political, economic or nationalistic. How then can a movement based on religious Kalimah be called deficient or limited in any way? Religious Kalimah is an all-embracing, all-inclusive Kalimah.

The second part of the Maulana's call is to prayer. Usually people underestimate it, and therefore, fail to appreciate its real significance.

Just as Kalimah enjoys the main position in one's thoughts and feelings, so does prayer in one's practical life.

The real significance of prayer lies in man's diverting all his attention to God and making contact with Him through sense-perceptions. Through them, the worshipper bows before his Lord, placing his forehead on the ground, he testifies to his own lowliness as opposed to God's exhalted nature. He presents himself as God's servant. He stands before God, bows down to Him, and prostrates himself before Him, in a practical demonstration of submission to God. It is when one humbles oneself before the Lord, that one is in a position to meet Him; for one discovers God on a level of humility, not on a level of pride and egotism. One's soul then undergoes such an experience that one can feel the blessing of God descending upon one.

Such an experience, which defies description gives a new dimension to human personality. The worshipper consciously realizes how helpless and powerless he is before God. Humility and modesty alone befits a servant of God. In the process, arrogance and haughtiness, which are the source of most evils, vanish into thin air.

Prayer, as is mentioned in the Quran, also keeps one away from evils and shameful practices. With every prayer, man expresses his servitude before God and promises to Him that he will lead his life as His devoted servant. It reminds him of the day of reckoning. If man is true to his words, his life can be transformed by them.

Remembrance, which is called Dhikr, forms an important aspect of prayer. To fill one's heart and mind with remembrances of God is to occupy it with such thoughts as befit it. Prayer thus serves to train people's thoughts and feelings in the best possible way.

Prayer also has psychological and social values; one can see the effects in economic, social and political life. The essence of prayer is to bow down one's head before God, and with one's heart, utter these words: "God, I have become yours, and you become mine."

Sparing time for the propagation of religion constitutes the third part of one's mission. People commonly misunderstand the word *Chilla*, which means forty days. It is nothing but a period fixed for training and being trained, and is fixed as the maximum time for one stint of outdoor missionary activity at a time. There is nothing mysterious or ritualistic about it. When one finds the truth, it is but natural to feel the urge to impart that treasure to one's brethren. This urge is manifested in one's willingness to spare time—even if it involves forty days—leaving all activities aside. One who has discovered the truth will not rest content with just being a true Muslim himself, but will want to announce it to the whole world. Such a mental state arising from a desire to reform all that comes in its path, takes on practical shape in the form of *Chilla*.

Maulana Ilyas attached great importance to this method of preaching. Besides being a means of conveying the message to others, it was a multi-purpose scheme meant to train, educate and reform. When a person undertakes long, arduous journeys in the path of Tabligh, he himself learns, while teaching others, and rectifies his own mistakes. Coming face to face with the pathetic plight of the people, he feels spurred on to intensify his efforts to bring them to the straight path. He makes sacrifices. He prays for them. It is then that he can truly taste the pleasures of a religious life. Then alone can he utter words which melt the hearts of the listener.

Making people come out of their homes is central to the Maulana's way of working, because this gives people the opportunity to quit their worldly atmosphere and go in search of a religious one. Only in an atmosphere free of worldly thoughts can there be true receptivity to the message conveyed. It becomes like a chain reaction. The listeners are imbued with the zeal to make others listen to them. This scheme of encouraging people to come forth has had amazingly successful results. Those who have not themselves experienced it, cannot imagine the transformation that takes place.

To set out to propagate the divine message as the prophet has enjoined is to stear one's feet along the path of God. Feet once sat on the path of truth will not be touched by hellfire. Those who perform the miracle of jumping into a pit of fire, without being hurt by the fire, actually rub certain substances over their bodies which protect their skin from fire. So the divine particles of dust which arise from this path and adhere to our bodies will neutralize the effects of fire in the next world.

This, however, should not create the impression that Maulana Ilyas and his followers, considered just the mobility of some groups, in the name of Tabligh, enough in itself to earn us salvation. It is, indeed the upsurge of religion which is aimed at, and not just the physical movement of the people. What the Hadith has to say regarding protection from hellfire will thus be applicable to us only if we can make religion a reality for others. The more our intentions are pure, the more we qualify for divine succour. The Maulana has thus ruled out the idea that the movement of certain chosen groups is desirable in itself. He once said: "Our method of working, lays emphasis upon taking people out of their homes in groups. The main advantage of this method is to encourage people to come out of a worldly and static atmosphere in order to enter a new, pure and dynamic one where there is much to foster the growth of religious consciousness. Besides, travel and emigration involve hardship, sacrifice and self-abnegation for the sake of God's cause, and thus entitle one to divine succour.

Stressing on the Basics

The Maulana described this method as the ABC of the Tabligh mission, but it does not mean that ABC and XYZ are far removed from one another. Those whose eyes are set on appearances are incapable of observing reality in depth. In fact, this method is like a drop of water which finally becomes an ocean. The difference between a drop of water and an ocean is one of degree. The drop is like the steam which an engine driver gets up for his locomotive. Without that, the engine cannot even start, let alone reach its destination. There has to be that first drop for the ocean to be formed. There has to be steam in the engine for it to move at all.

There are two ways of working. One is to draft the whole plan before the launching of the mission. Another is to start with the basics, the foundations. While the first method is adopted by the legislature, the second is adopted by a movement, for the first method will do the movement more harm than good. That is why messengers of God emphasized the basics in order that the foundation may take root. In the early period of Islam only the fundamentals were revealed for a long time. It was only with the advance of time that other things followed. Thus a solid foundation was gradually built, without which no edifice can be constructed.

From the Islamic point of view, it is by the grace of God that we are able to work on an individual or social level. Man takes certain initiatives which come to fruition only when God approves of and blesses them.

Once a person asked the Maulana why the Muslims were not entrusted with power on earth. He replied: "When you are not applying God's commandments and injunctions to yourselves when there is nothing actually to prevent you from doing so, how can you hope to have the administration of the world committed to your care?"

The Use of Pen

One day the Maulana said to one of his followers, who was a writer, "So far I have not approved of the use of the pen in this work, but now the time has come to use this medium. Not only have I not approved of it but I have also prohibited people from using it. But now I want them to write as much as they can. You must consult other senior members in this regard." They were consulted but they did not agree with his opinion. On hearing of their disagreement, the Maulana again observed: "Actually, in the beginning, we were in danger of being seriously misunderstood. People were not prepared even to listen to us. It was, in those circumstances, imperative that we approach them personally, and, by our example, impress upon them our objectives. If we had then taken recourse to writing, people would surely have misinterpreted the mission. And then, when its application went awry, they would have rejected it altogether as worthless. That is why we deliberately avoided the help of the news media. But now, owing to our devoted volunteers who have worked hard to spread the mission among the people, it has become as clear as the day. The people themselves are now flocking to us in order to learn more and more. We have a large number of devoted people who can be sent to any part of the country wherever the need arises. There is no point in our sticking to the initial method of working when the times have changed. I recommend therefore, that you take up your pens to further the cause of this mission." He commented a number of times that they functioned according to the capacities of the people at their disposal. "If we had people with a different set of abilities, we would have expanded our work in other directions too." His thoughts on the use of the written word, may be summarized thus:

"Whenever a new movement is launched, the most important task is that of proper introduction. The need is felt for the preacher to approach the congregation personally. But a time comes when the message becomes plain for all to grasp. Then there are no chances of misrepresentation. The main terms are fully understood by the people, and become a part of their consciousness. Then it is not so much the speaker's words being a source of introduction, as people's minds being already conditioned to the thoughts expressed, which makes it easier to convey the message. There is, therefore, no need for the reservations initially considered necessary."

Another thing is that there are many different aspects of a movement. In practice, the movement functions only in the field for which its workers are well-equipped. How can one succeed in realizing projects for which there are no efficient hands? The method adopted by the Maulana at the outset cannot be underestimated as a matter of fundamental principle, but the abilities of the workers that came to him also account in large measure for the way his mission took shape. With the spread of the movement, the work can also be expanded to other fields, as the workers are now more versatile than they were formerly. The Maulana once said something of great value. He said that one approach is through general training and education, whereas, in emergencies, something quite different is called for. The first method is that of the prophets—to train and educate in general; otherwise it is the situation and circumstances which dictate the method. It is self-evident that the first method is unvarying in value, while the second is subject to change from situation to situation. The Maulana did not underestimate the importance of literature. The issues that confront us on an academic level can only be properly presented and countered by the same weapon. In the Abbasid period, the publication of Greek literature aroused many new intellectual problems, which were adequately countered by the writings of the scholars of the time. Consequently, theology came into existence. Similarly, today, Islam is being challenged at various points by thoughts and issues that have to be countered on its behalf. The Maulana was fully aware of this necessity, but felt that this was a secondary matter and, as such, should be treated as a temporary emergency, and should not form part of the substance of religious teaching in general.

2

HAZRAT JI

Maulana Mohammed Yusuf, generally known to his followers as Hazrat Ji, was about to board a train from Lahore to Saharanpur. Lahore had been the last stage of a long missionary tour which had taken him as far as Dhaka and to many other cities in both West and East Pakistan. He had a very heavy and demanding schedule, but following in the footsteps of his father, Maulana Ilyas, he had never once thought of sparing himself. Now he was going home. But this was not to be, for on that fateful day, the second of April 1965, he suffered a heart attack which proved fatal. This was a tragedy, no doubt, but it was one about which he had never allowed himself to feel apprehensive. The Tabligh movement came before all.

Maulana Mohd Yousuf was born on 2nd March 1917. After the death of his father in 1944, he persevered in the same path for 21 years till the end. In this short span of time, a movement, which had started from teaching the illiterate Mewati Muslims the Kalimah and prayer, developed into a national and then an international movement. It influenced people from all walks of life, of diverse abilities and professions. A great achievement indeed, and quite unprecedented.

A contemporary of his, and a well-known scholar, Maulana Mohd Manzoor Nomani, has narrated how a Tabligh gathering was held in Moradabad only a few months after the death of Maulana Mohd Ilyas. At that time, the idea of sparing time for Tabligh had not become a common practice in areas other than Mewat. Maulana Mohd Yousuf delivered a speech after the morning prayer.

When it was over, some of the members began to exhort the people to register their names as participants in the outdoor religious activities of the movement. But only a few people came forward. For the dispatching of missionary parties to Bijnore, Chandpur and Rampur, not even a group of ten people could be formed. On learning of their apathy, Maulana Yousuf, who had gone inside the mosque after his speech, came back out, picked up the microphone and began thus: "Today you are reluctant to travel to such nearby places. A time will come when you will go to Syria, Egypt, Iraq, but by then your rewards will have diminished, because by that time such activity will have become common practice."

This had appeared to be a figment of imagination at that time, but now this dream has come true. The movement of Tabligh has spread its wings far and wide; not only to Muslim countries, but also to Europe, Japan and the U.S.A. It would no more be an exaggeration to state that at every moment, some group or the other is on the move, in some part of the globe.

Total Involvement

There are hundreds and thousands of people who had the opportunity to come close to Maulana Yousuf, and witness his deep involvement in his mission. A member of the audience in Lahore who attended the gathering that was held after the morning prayers, says: "The Maulana began his speech and continued for three solid hours with unflagging energy. It seemed as though some volcanic eruption had taken place which was melting the hearts of the listeners. This address ended at 8.30, then it was time for breakfast. As he sat down to eat, the Maulana began again. Amazingly enough, he resumed his speech with such vigour, variety of arguments, freshness and spontaneity, that it was hard to imagine that it was the same person who had just finished a three-hour speech.

"In this breakfast meeting, so engrossed was he in explaining his mission to the people, that he paid no attention to his food. When one of his colleagues offered him a cup of tea, he accepted it, but held it in his hand for about 15 minutes. On having his attention drawn to it, he poured this cold tea down his throat. Another cup of hot tea was offered with biscuits but again he held the cup in his hand for a long time and then drank it like water when it had turned cold. Now he got up to address another meeting. Although he knew beforehand that he had to address another meeting before noon, he did not take any rest. And this was no exception. Such was his routine."

One of his colleagues who knew him personally said that before going to make a speech the Maulana always turned to God to seek His help. And when he began, his absorption was total.

Once there was a gathering in Bhopal. At that time the Maulana was suffering from wounds on his thighs which bled even with the slightest movement. He had come to Bhopal in this condition and, as usual, refused to take rest. He made speeches at different gatherings, and as a result, the wounds worsened. After the gatherings in Bhopal, he travelled to a place which was 40-50 miles away, where a gathering had been organized. Although the Maulana was present, his colleagues decided not to allow him to speak on this occasion in order to save him from further exertion. A substitute for him was found. But when the speech was made the Maulana felt that it has been lacking in force and conviction, so he insisted on making one himself. Unable to sit up, he lay down on a bed, and began to speak. The wounds started bleeding. When one piece of cloth was drenched, it was replaced by another. In this way a number of pieces of cloth became soaked with blood. The Maulana ended his speech only when he had elaborated upon the relevant points. It was estimated that about half a kilo of blood had oozed out of the wound during this speech. But this devoted servant of God did not even care to know what was happening, let alone allow himself to be disturbed by it.

In any family, the person who knows the husband best is the wife. The Maulana's late wife had been suffering from tuberculosis, and towards the end, her condition had considerably deteriorated. But the Maulana could hardly spare a moment to look after her. Someone sent his wife to her, having advised her to talk to Maulana's wife with such sympathy that she should be induced to betray any grudges she bore against the Maulana. The lady talked to her for quite sometime. But the Maulana's wife did not utter a single word of complaint againt her husband. Instead, she defended him, saying, "he is so engrossed in his work, that he hardly has any time even to look after himself. I have myself told him not to worry about me. I am receiving treatment for my illness. If God were to bring us together in heaven we would have enough time to live in peace." Some months later she died while in prayer.

The Call

The Maulana's eagerness to lead people along the right path had turned to anguish. To him, faith involved trusting in God in all matters to the exclusion of all else. Once he said that working for this cause entailed a firm belief in God because it was He alone who could bring success. Man had to submerge his being within Him. He had to be fully convinced that in following the prophetic way alone lay the success of both the worlds.

"There are, two fields of struggle," he once said "One concerns the earth on which we live, and the other is the world of faith. The first type of struggle brings forth the fruits of our worldly labours. But it does not afford one any deep sense of happiness and contentment. The second type of struggle reaps dividends in the next world." To the Maulana, dominance on earth was subject to our leading truly Islamic lives. As he said, "Follow the pattern of the Prophet. Those who neither wish to follow his path themselves nor let others follow it, will be shattered by God as He does the shell of an egg. The super powers, to God, are not worth even a spider's web. It is only the deplorable lack of pure souls that has caused such spider's webs to grow.

"No sooner had the people reformed themselves through

the efforts of the Prophet, than God sent His scourge upon the Romans and Persians. Those who did not capitulate before Him perished by His wrath." Here are some excerpts from one of the Maulana's letters. "Man's success is in proportion to his inner resources. It is spiritual success and failure alone that matter. Worldly success and failure keep fluctuating. Men of position and power are reduced to nothing if that is the will of God and, conversely the resourceless have position and power conferred upon them."

"Those who have faith and do good deeds will have their failures turned by God into successes. Everything lies in the hands of God, He alone wields influence over everything in this world. When one truly loves and fears God, and is wholeheartedly willing to follow the path shown by the Prophet Mohammad, God will see to it that our initiatives are brought to fruition. Today people adhere to the outward form of religion, while the spirit is lost."

"The companions of the Prophet trod this path heart and soul. They devoted their whole lives to the propagation of this message. We must follow their pattern. We must expend all our energies on reaching the true path. We must make sacrifices of time and money, yet expect no return. We shall have to migrate for this cause when the call comes, and help those who have already chosen to tread it. The prayers of such people shall be answered like those of the Jewish Prophets. Just as God came to their help to overcome their enemies, so God will come to our rescue too. If this struggle is internationalized, God will bring revolution within the hearts of the people all over the world."

People believe that things come into being through a process of cause and effect. The Prophets showed us that everything is caused by God. If this reality were firmly fixed in people's minds, in the words of the Maulana, "our attention will be diverted from the markets to prayers, and the most difficult of jobs will be made easy by God." The Maulana laid most emphasis on impressing upon the minds of the people the importance of understanding the area of their struggle. There are some who consider agriculture, business and science as being the area in which to exert the utmost. There are others who depend upon elections to bring pressure to bear upon the government for the realization of their collective aims and goals.

The Maulana maintained that these material matters could be likened to bulbs and fans. Even if we direct all our efforts towards bulbs and fans, we cannot make them function; we have to operate the switch which activates them. Similarly it is contact with God alone which can bring our efforts to fruition in every field. Without this our best efforts are in vain.

Method of Working

The Maulana's method of working for this goal was very simple. It was to revive the activities of the mosques on the pattern of the early days of Islam. Movement and travel were greatly emphasized, as a means to make people truly religious. People were to be withdrawn for a time from their daily chores to share in the religious environment. There they were trained to urge others to follow the same path. And, when they returned home, they were expected to retain their impression for a long time. It was expected that the religious and spiritual lessons they had been taught, would be pursued by them in the mosques of their neighbourhood. This mosque-oriented life in itself, as the Maulana saw it, would ensure success in both the worlds.

He explained his point of view in a letter to one of his followers: "To learn to lead a truly religious life, whatever the sphere one belonged to, one was required to spare four months out of one's worldly engagements. During this period one had to preach the word of God to all those one came in contact with, on journeys to various places in and outside the country. The Prophet's companions had thrown themselves into the performing of this task with total dedication. Their activities centered on mosques, where they talked of the greatness of God which strengthened them in their faith. It was in the mosques that they learnt how to purify their actions. It was there that the fact that they were accountable to God for their deeds was indelibly impressed upon them. It was in the mosques also that the missionary groups were formed. People from all walks of life gathered to remember God in the mosques and came in contact with one another there. Today we mistakenly suppose that it is the money that we earn by our efforts that runs the mosques. The mosques, consequently, are full of material objects and devoid of spiritual wealth. The mosques at the time of the companions of the Prophet were not dependent upon businessmen and did not have such facilities as we have today. Still, they served as great training centres in individuals' and in social life. Their frequenters first reformed their own ways and then spared no efforts to initiate others into the same way of life. Now we must set ourselves the task of preparing others to share this responsibility of indoctrinating others with religious truths alongside their secular education. After having performed the outdoor activities they should not forget the learning they have gained in the process of teaching; and they must continue those activities in the mosques of their own areas. It is our bounden duty to draw their attention towards this gigantic task. At least one person in each family should devote a part of his time to this job. Such people should then work in unison. The local parties must visit different local mosques in turn to impart religious education to those assembled therein. This will create an environment for religious activities. Afterwards they should cover the mosques situated outside their own settlements. The mosques situated at a distance should be visited once a month and their stay there should be for at least for three days in the month. God will generously reward them for their three days work as if it were equal to 30 days. Those who devote three days to such work every month will be reckoned by God as having served for the whole year."

Shunning Publicity

The Maulana disapproved of the prevalent system of publicity. He writes in one letter: "In order to make this mission public, the advertising media, newspapers, advertisements, posters and so on should be avoided as far as possible, for the whole of our work is unconventional. The real way of working is to address people individually, to impart education by approaching people, and forming groups of people to work together."

The Maulana's concept of literature can be understood from the following excerpts:

"After reading the books on Hadith, one should recite passages from the Quran. While imparting religious learning one should avoid speaking on one's own. One should first recite the Quran, then read excerpts from the Hadith, then briefly comment on the meanings of the passages read aloud with the aim of stimulating in the people a desire to work for the cause. The Hadith books should be read in public as well as in private."

He shunned publicity so much that after his death, no copies of his letters could be found, in spite of the fact that the Maulana wrote letters frequently.

Call to Non-Muslims

So far as preaching among non-Muslims is concerned, he held the view that until the Muslims themselves were reformed, non-Muslims could find no appeal in our religion. Once he said: "Unless one has firm conviction and has moulded one's way of life accordingly, one fails to become a good Muslim morally, and he who does not become a good Muslim himself is ill-equipped to spread the message among others. To be good to others out of selfish motives is not an act of morality. Without sincerity of intention, our actions are bereft of any value. There are innumerable people who appear to be physically alive but are spiritually dead, because their actions are lacking in sincerity." That is why he considered it of prime importance to reform Muslims themselves.

Unity

The Maulana greatly stressed unity, integrity and concentrated effort. He advised the people even to travel together as far as possible. He attached great value to remaining united, but disapproved of forming parties as usually happened. The Maulana said, "We have no party, no formal type of organization, no office, no register and no funds. Our work is to be shared by all Muslims. That's why, according to the times, we have not formed our people into a separate Jama'at (party). We are just working on the pattern of the mosques where people come together from different walks of life and, after having said their prayers, return to their daily chores. In the same manner, we ask you to spare some time to train yourselves, and then go back to your daily duties. Once you have imbibed religion in its true spirit, the people of the world will approach you to acquire knowledge from you, and Insha Allah, one of these days, the leadership of the world will be conferred upon you."

In a speech he advises the preachers thus:

"When you visit someone in person with the aim of conveying the message to him, and you find him unfavourably inclined, you should cut short your visit and come back to pray for him. On your next visit, when you find him showing some interest, only then should you speak to him in detail. When you visit a religious scholar, you should ask only for his blessings. However, if you find him willing to hear you, you can briefly mention your work to him."

Prayer

The Maulana always concluded his speech with prayer. The word prayer as it is generally understood, is perhaps inadequate to recall fully what prayer meant to him. In seeking God's help through prayer, he aspired to establish direct contact with God, and so engrossed was he with his prayers that he seemed to be the embodiment of them. Those who have attended his gatherings say, "while he was praying it seemed that he had neither prayed before nor was he ever going to pray again in future. It was as if he would ask for all that he had ever wanted and say to God all that he had ever wanted to say in that one prayer, his psychic state, the contents of his prayer, his spontaneity coupled with the unparalleled force of his words, cast a spell on the audience. When the prayer was made in Urdu, the people would almost burst into tears.

On one such occasion, he asked forgiveness for his sins, salvation in the next life, predominance of religion in this world, and guidance for all mankind. The prayer was made as was fitting, not a single eye in the congregation remained dry. All tongues responded to his call, and hearts leapt with the poignancy of it. He was obsessed with one thing alone: the nagging feeling of having spent his life in vain — the feeling of having fallen short of the divine standard. "O, my God, forgive us for all of our inadequacies and failures, and guide us along the right path!"

Here is one prayer which is preserved on a tape:
"O, my God, forgive us for our sins. Forgive us for our lapses in carrying out the work as deserved by your cause. We have pathetically failed in fulfilling the mission of the prophets, and we have engaged ourselves in worldly pursuits. God, save us from the depths of degradation we have fallen into and guide us along the right path. We are grateful to You for having shown us Your path and granted us the service of Your cause. Accept from us the struggles that we have made and bless our efforts. May You, God, establish peace and justice all over the world, and bring to an end corruption and cruelty. Help all of us who have joined Your cause and answer our prayers."

A Divine Gift

The Maulana seemed to be a born speaker, and his unbounded zeal served to burnish this gift. After hearing his speeches, a religious scholar said, "It seemed that he had been endowed with a divine gift and that it was not an acquisition." It was wisdom, combined with the force with which he expressed himself. In his final days, he sometimes had to speak for eight hours continuously, and it is truly amazing that neither common men nor religious scholars ever found his lengthy speeches tedious. They were all concentration till the end. A large number of them appreciated his discourses to such an extent that they would note down the contents during the speech itself. It was astonishing that the listeners felt as though it were his first speech, as if it were full of pristine vigour and force.

An adherent who attended the Maulana on a journey writes: "The Maulana addressed many gatherings for hours together, till his throat swelled with the extreme exertion. The doctors insisted on his taking rest, but he would not oblige them. He continued to deliver speeches to every gathering that was organized on that occasion at the risk of aggravating the condition of his throat.

The style of his speeches was unique, and the intensity of his emotion would betray itself in physcial agitation—he would stand up and sit down repeatedly and pull his sleeves up and down as he spoke. The feeling that his struggle had not met with the intended result was so agonizing to him, that he would sigh and groan at which the hearts of his listeners would melt.

One of his followers observed that Hazrat Ji used to talk continuously for hours. He himself had attended five of his lectures in one day, one of which alone was of five and a half hour duration. It seemed like an endless sea of knowledge: the source of his inspiration was eternal and ever-flowing.

Taste for Learning

His taste for acquiring knowledge was immense. One of his colleagues has it that, the Maulana once told him he had bought sweets for himself only once. It was not because he had no money, but because he saved his money to buy books on the life of the Prophet Mohammad. Maulana Inamul Hasan, a friend and class fellow of the Maulana recounts how both of them had decided to keep awake at night to study. "It was arranged that one night the Maulana would keep awake for the first half of the night while I slept, and then, at midnight, he would waken me and give me a cup of tea so that I could study during the latter half of the night. Then he would go to sleep. The next day I did vice versa. One night the Maulana studied in the first half of the night and the second night I studied in the first half of the night, thus giving ourselves some variety. "In his later life at Basti Hazrat Nizamuddin, he had a busy schedule, but he had fixed a period of time every day to read and write.

An incident recounted by a religious scholar from Nadwa, Lucknow underscores this aspect of the Maulana. It seems that at a gathering addressed by the late Maulana Yousuf, there was pindrop silence for his words of wisdom and inspiration. Maulana Syed Abul Hasan Ali Nadwi, a great religious scholar, who was also present on this occasion, remarked, when the speech was at its zenith, that he would not be guilty of dishonesty if he were to swear that there was no religious scholar in the whole of the Muslim world who could speak so convincingly and with the same degree of faith and conviction as Maulana Yousuf. (1386 AH)

3

UMMAH-NESS
Islamic Brotherhood

(This is the text of a speech delivered by Maulana Mohammad Yousuf three days before his death, on 30 March 1965, at Rawalpindi, Pakistan)

"Listen! I am not feeling well. I have not been able to sleep the whole night. But I find it necessary to speak. Those who pay heed to the will of God and do good works will be rewarded by him. Those who do not will suffer the consequences of their wrong-doing.

"The Prophet and his companions took great pains to establish the Ummah (the community of believers). The enemies have always attempted to divide them. Muslims fall a prey to their manoeuvring and have often remained severely at odds with one another. There was a time when they were united and by virtue of their unity they outweighed the whole world, in spite of the fact that they were only a few lakhs in number. There were no brick houses, no brick mosques, there was no means of even lighting up the Masjid-e-Nabavi (the Prophet's mosque). It was as late as the ninth year of Hijra that the Prophet's mosque was lighted by Tamim Dari, who had accepted Islam in that year. By this time, almost the whole of Arabia had entered the fold of Islam. Various nations, various languages, various tribes had come together to form a single united whole. Only then was the mosque lighted up. The divine light brought by the Prophet had spread not only over Arabia, but all around it as well. In whatever direction this faithful little band of followers proceeded, people fell at their feet. This Ummah was established only after a great sacrifice of the interests of family, party, nation, country, language and so on. Even family affairs were not given prime importance because everything had literally been subordinated to the will of God and His prophets. Ummah can be formed only when all relations and acquaintances take on secondary importance. When Muslims were one community, the murder of even one Muslim was enough to shake all of them. Now the killings of hundreds and thousands of them goes unnoticed.

"Ummah is not the name of a group belonging to one nation or one place, but is formed rather of people of various lands and climes joined together into one whole. Those who consider a particular nation or a particular people as their own are guilty of destroying the Ummah by breaking it up into separate entities. The efforts of the Prophet and his companions towards unity are then rendered null and void. It is Muslims themselves who have done the Ummah to death. It was only later that others played their part. If Muslims were to unite once again, no power in the world could harm them. Even atom bombs and rockets could not vanquish them. But if national and racial prejudices are allowed to creep in, then even arms and armies cannot save us.

"Muslims are being subjected to oppression throughout the world because they are disunited. Feeling overwhelmed by the horror of the whole thing, my heart is ready to break. As you know, we have plunged ourselves into the plight we are in because we are divided. People have almost forgotten the difficulties the Prophet faced in bringing Ummah into being. For a community to lay claim to the divine succour, worship and the imparting of religious knowledge are not by themselves sufficient. Take the case of Abu Muljim, the murderer of the fourth Caliph. When people in a fit of anger rushed to avenge the murder by cutting his tongue off, he said 'Do whatever you will, but spare my tongue to enable me to utter God's name till my last breath.' Yet the Prophet had foretold that Ali's murderer would be one of the most hard-hearted and one of the most wretched members of his community. And so far as imparting religious knowledge is concerned, Abul Fazl and Faizi, the Emperor Akbar's courtiers, were so competent and well-versed that they could perform the feat of writing a complete commentary of the Holy Quran without using those letters of the alphabet which have points. But they were the very ones who led Akbar astray and perverted the religion itself. How then can worship and religious learning alone suffice to elicit the divine succour?

"The great warriors Shah Ismail Shaheed and Syed Ahmed Shaheed and their followers were, by all accounts, true believers. When they reached the frontier in Afghanistan in order to establish Islamic rule, the local people acknowledged them as their leaders, but Satan was close by to turn them against the newcomers. 'How can you allow the outsiders to have the upper hand in your affairs?' he whispered into their ears. The people succumbed to the temptation of Satan and revolted against them, putting many to death and expelling the rest from the country. Thus they broke the unity on purely regional grounds. God then placed them under the yoke of the English as a punishment.

"Remember! The words, 'my nation, my region, and my people' all lead to disunity, and God disapproves of this more than anything else.

"Ummah can be formed only when all its groups fully dedicate themselves to the task, ignoring all the differences between them. Remember that it is social evil that causes disunity. When one person wrongs another, subjects him to oppression or humiliates him, disunity is close at hand.

"I tell you that worship alone is not sufficient to keep the Ummah intact. Its unity entails reforming our ways vis a vis those we come in contact with, paying them their dues, according them proper respect, and sacrificing our own interests in favour of community interests. Consider how the Prophet and his companions endured the unendurable for the sake of uniting people together around one goal.

"During the caliphate of Umer, an enormous sum in

booty and tax was collected and brought to him. A meeting was held to decide on the method of distribution. It was at a time when Ummah had been established and all were united. People from various tribes participated in the meeting. They arrived at the decision that the following system should be adopted. The tribe to which the prophet belonged was to receive the highest share, next would come Abu Bakr's tribe and then Umer's. In this manner Umer's tribe came thrid on the list. This proposal was put before Umer, but he did not agree to this. He said, 'We owe everything to the Prophet, so we should let him establish the criterion. Those related to him should first receive the greatest share, and then other tribes should be classed according to their relationship with his tribe.' By this standard, Umer's tribe lagged far behind, and was entitled to receive a much smaller share in comparison. It was such selfless people as these who had brought the Ummah together.

"It is incumbent upon us to remain united whatever the cost. The Prophet is reported to have said: 'On the day of Judgement a certain person would be brought before God to be judged, and although he had performed all forms of worship in the world, he would stand condemned. He would wonder what it was that he was being punished for. He would be told that it was due to such words of his as had caused friction in Ummah that he had been brought to this state. Afterwards another person would be brought, who had worshipped God far less in comparison to the former person. But he would be amply rewarded. In astonishment, he would ask: 'For which of my deeds have I been rewarded so generously.' He would be told that on some occasion he had done something or spoken some words, which had helped to bring the community together, and that it was his good words that had brought him all the reward.

"The tongue indeed plays a large part in connecting or splitting asunder a community. If the tongue can utter such words as create disharmony in a community, the tongue can as well utter such words as unite the hearts of people who were formerly antagonistic to one another. It is, therefore, necessary to keep our tongues in check. One should always bear in mind that God listens to every word we utter; this awareness alone can act as a constraint.

"Two Medinan tribes, the Aus and Khazraj, were torn with civil and tribal feuds and dissensions and, as a result, had been severely at odds with one another for centuries. By virtue of their acceptance of Islam they had united in a peerless brotherhood. On seeing this, the Jews plotted against them in order to provoke them into clashing once again. At a gathering where people from both tribes were present, a conspirator recited provocative verses with the intention of arousing their negative emotions. The plot succeeded. Both the groups first engaged in heated exchanges, then fell to shedding the blood of their brethren. When the Prophet was informed, he rushed to the spot and asked them, "Would you shed the blood of your brethren while I am alive?" Then he made a brief but poignant and moving speech before them. Both sides realized that they had simply played into the hands of Satan. They embraced one another and wept at having been led astray. It was on this occassion that this verse was revealed:

"Ye, who believe, fear God as He should be feared, and die not except in a state of Islam" (Quran 2:102).

"When man keeps God constantly in his thoughts, he will always fear Him and try to follow Him in every detail. Satan will then never find a chance to tempt him to evil ways, and the community will be spared friction.

"'And hold fast, all together, by the rope which God (stretches out for you) and be not divided among yourselves and remember with gratitude God's favour on you. For ye were enemies and He joined your hearts, in love so that by His grace, ye became brethren; and ye were on the brink of the pit of fire and He saved you from it.' (Quran 3:104)

"'Let there arise out of you a band of people inviting to all that is good, enjoining what is right and forbidding what is wrong. They are the ones to attain felicity.' (Quran 3:104)

"The ideal Muslim community is one that is united,

strong and prosperous; it encourages all that is good; enjoins what is right; and forbids what is wrong.

"'Be not like those who are divided amongst themselves, and fall into disputation after receiving clear signs. for them is a dreadful penalty.' (Quran 3:105)

"In Islam great emphasis is laid on unity. All the forms of worship are aimed at bringing people together, while bad deeds divide one from another the faces of those who are guilty of the heinous crime of dividing people shall appear black on the day of judgement.

"'On the Day when some faces will be (lit up with) white, and some faces will be (in the gloom of) black. To those whose faces will be black, will be said: Did you reject faith after accepting it? Taste then the penalty for rejecting faith. But those whose faces will be (lit with) white— they will be (in the light of) God's mercy: therein to dwell (forever) (Quran 3:106-107).

"All these verses were revealed at the point when the Jews had succeeded in their attempt to cause a rift between members of the Ansar (the Medinan new converts). The latter were momentarily influenced by their insinuations. Civil war and friction in the Muslim community has been likened to unbelief. Those guilty of it will be liable to severe chastisement in the next world. The only way to counteract such attempts on the part of the enemies, is to continue towards the goal of bringing people together in the mosques, to organize religious meetings and discussions aimed at strengthening one in one's faith and making one conscious of one's duties of spreading the message among the ignorant. Constant remembrance of God alone can help us to resist Satanic temptations.If we always remembered the fact that God is watching over us every moment, we would be cautious of our words and deeds. If we are to achieve unity we must win over our enemies, however strong they may be. The moment we become disunited, others will hold sway over us.

"The Quran strongly condemns all those things that create misunderstanding between the people.

"'Secret counsels are only inspired by the Evil one, in

order that he may cause grief to the believers; but he cannot harm them in the least, except as God permits.' (Quran 58:10)

"The believers are brethren. Make peace among your brethren and fear God, so that you may be shown mercy.'

"'Believers, let no man mock another man, who may perhaps be better than himself. Let no woman mock another woman, who may perhaps be better than herself. Do not defame one another, nor call one another by nicknames. It is an evil thing to be called by a bad name after embracing the true faith. Those that do not respect are wrong doers.' (Quran 49:11)

"'Believers, avoid most of suspicion, for in some cases suspicion, is a crime. Do not spy on one another, not backbite one another.' (Quran 49:12)

"The collective community of Islam should be supreme over groups or nations. It would be expected to act justly and to try through compromise to avoid quarrels, for peace is better than fighting.

"The enforcement of Muslim Brotherhood is the greatest social ideal of Islam. On it was based the Prophet's sermon on his last pilgrimage, and Islam cannot be completely realized until this ideal is achieved.

"Mutual ridicule ceases to be amusing when there is arrogance or selfishness or malice behind it. We may laugh *with* people, to share in the happiness of life: We must never laugh *at* people in contempt or ridicule. In many things they may be better than ourselves. In our mission we exhort people to learn the virtues of modesty, and when they come to possess them, surely they will succeed in both the worlds.

"Defamation may consist in speaking ill of others by spoken or written words, or in acting in such a way as to suggest the culpability of some person whom we are not in a position to judge. All these things ill-accord with the serious purpose which Muslims should have in life.

"Most kinds of suspicions are baseless and are to be avoided, and some are crimes in themselves, for they do cruel injustice to innocent men and women. Spying, or inquiring too curiously into people's affairs means either idle curiosity, and is therefore futile, or suspicion carried a stage further, which almost amounts to sin. Slandering others falls into the same category. If slander is baseless it can range from being purely mischievous, to being poisoned with malice, in which case it is a sin added to sin.

"We must accord due respect to Muslims. This can take place only when we step down to the lowly position of a slave of God.

"If we learn the lessons of true humility when we know consciously that we are not worthy of being honoured while others are, then can we rest assured that unity is secured.

"We have to make sacrifices of our interests in this path. Power rests in the hands of God, not in the hands of mortals. When we fully submit ourselves to Him, He grants a share of it, if He so wills. And if we rebel against Him, He can take away even what we already possess, just as He did with the rebellious Jews who called themselves the chosen people of God. God does not judge people by relationships. It is our deeds alone which matter.

"My friends, exert with all your might in this cause of bringing unity to our people, through faith and self reform. This community should become one which worships God as is proper and is humble towards its fellowmen, which gives respect to others, is obedient to God, and whose members' lives are imbued with truth and justice. Even if people in only one small place fully devote themselves to the spreading of this message, it will in time become the order of the day.

"It is high time that we formed groups to visit various places and did our best to serve this cause. In this way by the grace of God, nothing could come in the way of spreading the message.

4

TWO DAYS IN NIZAMUDDIN

The Upper India Express was charging along at full speed. The green fields on both sides, the lakes and rivers overflowing with water were a delight to the eye. The beauty of the hills and dales, the slopes and the heights, the land and the water made no difference to the train, however, for it continued to speed along unceasingly, ignoring the minor stations as if it were destined to continue its journey for ever.

It occurred to me at this point that the journey of a seeker of truth somewhat resembles it. The charms and delights of the world come before him to tempt and seduce him to the ways of the world, but he refuses to be affected by them. Comforts and luxuries lure him, but he goes on his way without pausing. Matters of minor significance confront him, but his vision is not obstructed by them. He suffers setbacks in life, but that does not weaken him in his resolve. A seeker of truth is not like a stranded person in an aimless world. There is a goal that he has set himself and a destination that he is sure of. How can he then waste his time on the way by engaging himself in anything inferior to the goal he has set for himself? He will continue to proceed on his journey till he reaches his destination.

It was August 14, 1966. At 10 O'clock in the morning we arrived at our destination—Bangla Wali Masjid, situated near the tomb of Nizamuddin Aulia. This mosque has been famous as the centre of the reform movement for decades. There was a time when this place, far from the town, was sparsely populated. But now it bustles with life. The place is known as Basti Hazrat Nizamuddin, now a

53

part of Delhi Corporation. When Maulana Ilyas started his mission, his voice was as unfamiliar and unpopular as this place was at one time. Today a crowd of people are attracted to this mission and it has become the centre of a world movement. We can liken this centre to the heart. Just as the blood circulates from the heart throughout the body, then returns to the same place, so do the people going out from this place come back to it to recharge themselves spiritually so that they may continue their journey onwards with renewed vigour. This movement has a beginning, but has no end. It is boundless and endless.

People from far and near, from a diversity of lands and climes come together at this point. The congregation is of rich and poor, of young and old, of educated and illiterate.

What is it that brings myriads of people flocking to this place? This is the first question that strikes a new-comer. The answer is not long in coming to him, for as he joins in the programme, listening to the speeches and heart-felt prayers, and saying Amen to them, he can feel an extraordinary property possessing his heart and mind, just like magic. There is some irresistible force that draws him closer and closer to the truth of the matter. His own personal experience tells him why this place is thronged with people from far and near, from home and abroad.

I was asleep in a room in the upper storey of the mosque. The voice of the alarm wakened me up at half past three O' clock. The activities at the Tabligh centre had commenced. People got up and carried out their ablutions to be ready for Tahajjud (after-midnight prayer). Some engaged themselves in reciting the Quran; while others were praying for the improvement of Ummah (the community of believers), lying in prostration until the call to prayer was announced by a Muezzin (crier). About 300 men stood in rows to perform their dawn prayers.

When the prayer had finished, an announcement was made for people to stay, as a speech was going to be made shortly, its topic being, 'The Relationship between Religion and the World'. Simple words, spontaneity, striking, familiar, immediate similes, psychological expressiveness aimed at exciting religious zeal, a simple but forceful logic understandable even to the common man, far from the high flown words of religious speeches and free from the boredom of a sermon—these were, in short, the very fabric of the morning speech. It continued till the sun rose high. But the speech was so appealing that none of the listeners would leave before the end. When it was over, people were requested to offer their services and join the Jama'at that was due to leave town in order to spread the message among others. This programme came to an end at half past eight.

Now it was time for breakfast for the entire community. After breakfast, another meeting was arranged to impart religious knowledge which dwelt on forming a proper relationship with the Lord and trusting Him alone in all our affairs. This meeting concluded with prayers. The Chief (Emir) prayed, to which the others said Amen. The powerlessness of man and the all-powerfulness of God was emphasized. Feelings of love and fear for God so touched people's hearts as to make them cry. After this prayer, the despatching of missionary groups was attended to. Lists of those who had offered their services for this work were drawn up according to the areas to which they were to be despatched. The names of those people who were undertaking the journey were called out one by one, and each in turn came up to the chief to shake hands with him and receive his blessings before he departed. Such a poignant scene evoked memories of the Prophet sitting in the Masjid-e-Nabawi, exhorting people and sending them out in groups to propagate the message to those who were ignorant. The Emir shook hands with each of them and wished them well with the invocation: "I entrust you to God and pray for you. May God accept our humble services towards His path." Even a lame person offered himself and came limping to shake hands before he left. Another took along his 10 year old child. Those who witnessed the scene could not but be impressed.

This part of the programme ended at half past 12 O'clock. It was time for lunch. After that, some time was set aside for rest. At three O'clock the prayer was said. Again lessons in religious knowledge were given. The Asr (Afternoon) prayer was offered. Between Asr and Maghrib (sunset prayer) a long speech was made, then after Maghrib, the speech continued. Then the people withdrew to have dinner. After dinner the speech was resumed and ended only at midnight.

The programme mentioned above was not one meant for some special occasion. Rather this was the routine. Other movements and missions follow such a busy schedule only on special occasions. But at this religious centre, this very full programme is followed right throughout the year.

Hundreds of people are engaged in such wholesome activities as lessons in religious learning, remembrance of God, heartfelt prayers, recall of our duties to man, the practice of courtesy and so on. In short, a spiritual ambience is engendered the whole day long. This spiritual environment is the first thing that attracts the newcomer. He is also struck by the difference between this centre and the centres of other parties, be they religious or secular in character. Almost invariably such centres are eventually reduced to mere offices. The spirit of devotion and dedication with which they should be imbued gives way to routine, lifeless activities which are repeated, without meaning, day in and day out.

It is this difference that calls to mind the mosque of the Prophet. In the days of the Prophet and his companions, the Masjid-e-Nabawi was the centre of the Islamic movement. This centre was not, however, an office of ritual, routine activities like those favoured by the religious parties of modern times. It was the centre of Islam and of Islamic life itself, where prayers were held in remembrance of God, people gathered together to remember God, to turn to Him, to help their fellowmen, to recite the Quran and Hadith, to contemplate ways and means to propagate the message of Islam. On entering the Prophet's mosque, one felt as if one had reached an oasis after being exposed to extremes of climate. The Prophet's mosque of that time was not a grand building with every comfort. On the contrary, what was special about it was the pure Islamic environment which attracted people from far and near. There one could see real concern among the people to propagate the message of God, there one could see in the lives of the people the Quran being practised in the real sense of the word. Whoever attended the gatherings of the Prophet's mosque could not help being impressed.

Bangla Wali Mosque has been successful in creating just such an environment for more than a quarter of a century. It is a revival of one aspect of the Prophet's Sunnah, the like of which is hard to find in the recent past. In this world, there is no dearth of offices set up in th name of Islam. But an Islamic Centre on the pattern of Masjid-e-Nabavi is very rare. This fact in itself makes it worthy of the promised divine succour. It is related that Syed Ataullah Shah Bukhari, the great religious scholar, once visited this place, was so impressed by the activities of the mosque, that he observed in one of his speeches: "I thought that Nizamuddin Aulia had passed away. But I have learnt that he still lives on. I have renewed my faith during my stay here. Whosoever wishes to do the same should visit this place."

In order to understand the method that is adopted by this movement, we need to go back to its beginning. During my visit to the centre, while I was conversing with an associate of this mission, an elderly person who, by his appearance, seemed to be an illiterate villager, sat next to me. When one of my colleague casually mentioned shahadah (martyrdom), the villager added in a calm and dignified tone, "particularly when death occurs in the path of propagating the divine message." This remark of the villagers tells us that those who devote themselves to this mission, even if they be illiterate villagers, acquire a certain degree of enlightenment and wisdom.

I turned to him out of curiosity to find out who he was. He was a Mewati who had joined this movement at the age of eighteen through the inspiration of Maulana Ilyas. Since then he has never looked back.

This Mewati missionary had now grown old, bearded and of browner skin, and his simple and confident words made me feel as though I were in the presence of one of the companions of the Prophet. I listened to him with rapt attention just as an obedient student does to his kind teacher. I still regret that our conversation was interrupted and we had to separate.

He recounted the whole story of how Maulana Ilyas had been confronted with stiff resistance by unruly Mewati villagers when he attempted to reform them, and how on one occasion, in return for his exhortations, he had received a hard blow, as a result of which he had collapsed. The way he won the hearts of this barbarous people is a long story which has already been mentioned in the first chapter. To be brief, Maulana Ilyas realized from his experience that until the Mewatis were separated from their environment, the intended result could not be achieved. They were, therefore, brought to stay in mosques for a period of time in order to be exposed to the Islamic environment. Free from the worries and concerns of their daily chores, they proved to be more receptive to the message than could ever have been expected. The Bangla wali mosque became a practical centre where this method was applied to all those who gathered there. The Islamic environment is manifest there for all the twenty-four hours of the day. There is only one topic which dominates all conversation—the establishment of a proper relationship with God, because it is in God's hands that all power rests.

An Active Training Camp

The Tabligh missionaries aim at creating in the mosques they visit the same spiritual atmosphere that is found in Bangala Wali Mosque. During their visit to a mosque, they first go round the neighbourhood and invite people to the mosque. When the people have gathered they first have to say their prayers, then they are asked to recite parts from the Quran. Afterwards passages from the Hadith are read out to them, then they are helped to learn certain prayers by heart. They are told the rewards of good deeds and are reminded of their religious responsibilities. After they have reformed themselves to a certain extent, they are exhorted to spare some time to teach others what they have learnt. After understanding the implications of religion they should set out to make others understand. That is the most important part of the training. This method has worked wonders. Many who were steeped in ignorance have reformed their lives in its wake. They do not rest content at their personal reform but burn with zeal and ambition to reform others as well — to bring others to the same straight path which they have found for themselves.

Another feature peculiar to Tabligh is that, despite the change in leadership, its work has not slackened since its inception; rather it is on the increase. No movement can claim this distinction in modern history.

The history of modern parties shows that in the initial stage, they succeed in influencing people and attracting great minds, but that before long their work comes to a standstill. The people who had joined at the outset of the movement remained their only asset. No movement of modern times shows the capacity to continue to influence people on an intellectual plane. Although such movements seem to prosper even in the second phase so far as membership numbers are concerned, this success is not of the same nature as the original one. It almost assumes the form of a business, and the goal is relegated to the background.

The Tabligh movement enjoys a special advantage over other movements in that its appeal is enduring even today, and it has considerably expanded its horizons. People take part in its programmes with increasing interest and the numbers of new people coming to its fold are ever-increasing. The change in the lives of such people is pronounced, and the propagation of the message is on the increase.

Usually movements and parties are a product of their own time and circumstances. Although they claim to have derived their goal from eternal truths and use similar terms to express their aims and objectives, they are set in the present — a reaction to the circumstances. But the Tabligh work far from being something of momentary significance is based on eternal truths. It is eternal values that concern this movement. Its appeal is to human nature which is not subject to change. While external circumstances are in a state of flux, issues which initially seemed important tend to lose their charm. So a movement based on current issues can never have a lasting appeal. It can only find its place in the storehouse of history. Since the Tabligh movement is based on the demands of human nature, its appeal is lasting, and, so long as its people continue to carry on the work with sincerity of intention, the appeal will last, no matter how circumstances may change.

After Nizamuddin I stopped on my way at Aligarh. I was surprised to find hundreds of students who had undergone a transformation through the efforts of Tabligh workers over the last few years. There was a markedly different attitude towards religion then than there had been when I went there a few years ago. The students who were known for having disregarded religion under the influence of western culture and education could now be seen going to the mosque for their daily prayers; they visit the Nizamuddin Bangla Wali Mosque, to perform chillas. At times it becomes difficult to distinguish them from the students educated in Arabic schools. They have become more courteous and show more respect for one another than before. Even before leaving for the examination halls, they go to the mosque to pray to God to help them. There has never before been such a spiritual atmosphere in Aligarh, although theology has always been taught as a compulsory subject at the university.

Considering the transformation that the students at Aligarh Muslim University have undergone, a solution to the grave problems facing our country's younger generation is obviously in sight. The main problem is one of safeguarding our youth against the harmful influences of secular education. Nowadays the acquisition of a secular education on modern lines has become an inescapable necessity. This is not only because economics and allied subjects have come to the fore in the world of learning, but because, in the words of the Quran, it is the power of the day', and it is our duty to acquire it so that we may construct a worthy and stable national life. However, such traditions as have come to be associated with secular education either lead to atheism or, at best, to a loss of religious interest, and worldly goals are relentlessly pursued to the detriment of moral and religious values. However, the present environment at Aligarh brings an element of hope to this scene in that it shows us the way to discharge our duties. We can now help our young men to acquire a religious education side by side with a secular one; Tabligh provides a religious environment where they can be indoctrinated in religious beliefs and practices without this in any way being an obstacle to their studies. It is my personal experience that those students who devote a part of their time to religious pursuits do not lag behind their secular classfellows. They pass their examinations with good marks because, once religion has entered their lives, it acts as an intellectual stimulus and makes them more serious and more conscious of their duties. As a result, they save much time which would otherwise be wasted in fruitless activities. Their attitude towards life changes in its wake. They organize their lives more systematically and with a greater sense of responsibility, all of which enables them to carry out their work more efficiently. And God indeed blesses their efforts.

The Tabligh work has now spread all over Europe and America. Groups of volunteers are going abroad to spread the message, while people from abroad throng to the centre here to avail of the spiritual environment that prevails here.

Tabligh centres have been set up in many countries where, besides part-time volunteers, many other people have dedicated themselves to this mission on a full-time basis. Many of the students who go abroad to receive higher education prefer to keep in touch with the Tabligh volunteers during their stay, as this helps to keep them from falling under the pernicious influences of western apostasy.

Today the whole Muslim world has thrown itself into the field of secular education and our finest brains are receiving education in secular institutions. Were such students to keep in touch with the missionaries, they would surely escape any harmful influence. Two great benefits are to be gained through such contacts between students and missionaries, without their economic interests being in the least affected. Not only are baneful influences kept at bay, but the message can thus be better spread at home and abroad. Once students are trained they can continue to take up the task by sparing some time from their business or service, depending upon what course they have embarked upon after completing their education. If this plan is successful, the same process can be repeated once again, Insha Allah, which occurred in Arabia in the early period of Islam when Muslim merchants travelled to all the corners of the globe, making commerce a means of spreading the divine message.

The Tabligh people belive in conveying the message by means of personal approach: through conversation, speech, meetings and so on. They undertake journeys to convey these thoughts and ideas directly to the congregation. The only part the press plays in this mission is the publication of certain books, for example on the sayings of the Prophet and his companions and on the virtues of good deeds, etc. These books provide the missionaries with material for their speeches, and they are read out at congregations in order to import education to the assembly. Notwithstanding the major role of the press in modern times, its role in this instance is nominal. The Tabligh organizes huge gatherings every year such as no other party can manage to do, but they neither publish advertisements, handbills and posters, nor is any announcement made ,by loudspeaker. Hundreds and thousands of people have involved themselves in this work but no magazine is issued to bring them together, to educate them, or to give them instructions. I personally know that on one occasion when an editor of a certain newspaper published reports about a gathering that was being organized, the senior members went and met the editor to protest about it.

No doubt, holding such views will appear to be verging on fanaticism, but this firm attitude has brought about a high degree of efficiency which no other movement can claim to possess. It is a fact that when someone is advocating his beliefs and ideas to others in person, his words bear the whole force of his personality. There is sweetness in his words, feeling in his style and conviction in his tone. Moreover, when this conversation takes place in a religious milieu, that lends further emphasis to it. It is on a parallel with just listening to the sound-track of a play on the radio, as compared to being present in the theatre while it is being staged. The same difference is to be found between conveying the message through the news media and in making a personal approach.

There are, moreover, further advantages to this personal approach. It is possible, for example, to change the style of the speech to suit the needs of the audience. This is just not possible if the message is imparted through the medium of books or magazines. In one of the speeches made at Nizamuddin, it was related that at a certain place a juggler was making his monkeys perform. When the Tabligh people saw him, they went up to him to invite him to join in the prayers with them, but he refused. They came back in despair and said that they had done their best to persuade him but he would not rlent. Then three more people followed them. They said to him, "Sir, why are you spoiling your life by making these monkeys dance? In the next world God's angels will make you dance to the same tune." The juggler was moved. He listened to them seriously, then followed them to the mosque, tied the monkeys outside it, and himself entered the mosque to say his prayers.

Similarly, a preacher who resorts to oral methods has another advantage, that is, if his congregation finds it difficult to understand his message, he can illustrate it by means of practical examples which bring the point home.

The third benefit of the personal approach is that through contacts and exchanges of views, the missionary himself gains a great deal: new ideas, new ways of expression, and an access to the minds of the people, all of which helps him greatly to frame the messge in a manner that others can understand. In the process, the style of expression becomes simpler and more real. It becomes lucid and spontaneous, and this certainly has a greater appeal for the listeners than the written word.

During my stay at the centre, I heard the prayers of the chief of the Tabligh: one sentence of which ran like this: "May God bless our religious activities and activate us in every sphere connected with religion." This shows that they are not merely concerned with the revival of Kalima and prayers, but have set their sights on the revival of the whole of religion.

The only difference between Tabligh and other religious movements lies in the method of functioning — irrespective of the fact that others may regard something as part of religion while its members do not, or that others consider a certain part in need of being revived with which they do not necessarily agree.

It is generally known that Tabligh is concerned with Kalimah and prayer. In actual fact, it is a movement of faith and conviction; faith in the unseen realities, faith in God. Maulana Ilyas aptly called this movement a movement of faith. The Tabligh people firmly believe that the external factors which are apparently at work in life have no inherent power, and that all power rests with God, who is behind outward appearances. Because people usually tend to believe in forms which are visible — and we cannot do away with forms — we hve to encourage them to stop putting their trust in mere externals, and concentrate their minds on the superior reality.

The uninitiated profess that all things can work without recourse to God, whereas there is nothing which can actually work without the will of God. We have, therefore, to purify our hearts of all thoughts of misdirected trust in objects, save God; only then can our actions be acceptable to God. This makes it clear that the difference between Tabligh and other movements is not one of a limited or a broader concept of religion. On the contrary, it lies in the definition of arenas in which to exert their energies towards the establishment and revival of religion. There are some who regard the arena of their struggle as being Parliament House or an election campaign. On the contrary, the Tabligh people bring us to the point of placing our total trust in God who has power over all things. They exhort us to seek help from Him alone in all matters.

By establishing our relations with God, we receive all, as everything is in God's hands: it is He who has the upper hand in all events.

The Tabligh mission holds that it is God who is the cause of the causes; who determines our destinies, who nourishes and sustains, who confers power on or withholds it from whomsoever He will. All power belongs to Him. To expend our energies, therefore, on objects other than God is like trying to light a room by struggling with bulbs instead of with the switches. Since the predominance of divine religion as well as of the believers is associated with the cause which are in God's hand, so also can it be realized by pleasing God and making ourselves worthy of divine succour. The circumstances of the world will change in our favour only when we wholeheartedly submit to His will. Another advantage of Tabligh comes from its having based itself on faith rather than on reason. There are two ways of laying stress upon the importance of any cause. One is through the mind, and the other is through the heart. The former approach has recourse to reason and logic in order to prove the truth, while the latter approach plays on the emotions and feelings to convince the listener.

Those who have a knowledge of philosophy can understand how difficult and delicate the former path is. In actual fact, some hold, that it is not only difficult to prove or disprove anything on rational and logical grounds, but that it is impossible to prove anything by reason, even in this age of reason. If any rational movement has ever succeeded, it is not by dint of logical arguments, but because, by chance or by accident, it contained certain emotional aspects as well. We can furnish some instances from Socialism, Democracy, Evolution and so on. It is a fact that Socialism, up till now, has yet to be established by the standards of pure reason. Democracy has been exposed to innumerable objections, to which no satisfactory answer has yet been given. The theory of biological evolution, from the academic point of view, has so many flaws that it can at best be described as a belief rather than a theory. The success of these theories does not lie in their being rational and logical arguments, but in their having benefited from an emotional environment which already existed.

To prove something by means of pure logic and reason is indeed to attempt to catch a phoenix which has yet to exist. But there are other factors which we can put to good use. They are nature and tradition. It is no exaggeration to say that, even today, nature and tradition shape the personalities of almost 99 percent of the people.

Those who are born Muslims have an extra element in their favour; that is, they are brought up in the Muslim tradition, and in most cases they are imparted religious education in their childhood. At an unconscious level, at least, the religious outlook has a firm hold upon them. They might outwardly appear irreligious but, owing to the nature and tradition that they have inherited, in their inner selves, almost all are Islamic. The hold is usually upon their feelings and not upon their beliefs. That is why they respond to the impassioned appeals made by the missionaries. They hear the details of heaven and hell, their hearts are moved, the chords of their inner feelings are struck by means of prayer, even avowedly irreligious people break down and cry, deeply touched. Their appeal may not be endowed with reason, but it has an ecstatic value in it. And gradually the unconscious self comes to dominate when it is regularly exposed to such voices and is reborn. The greatest secret of success of the Tabligh mission lies in their exploiting the inherent emotional basis rather than attempting to catch the rational phoenix. This procedure may appear non-religious but the success rate is cent percent.

Now the question arises as to *w hat* the Tabligh is doing. Is it right, and does it suffice for the revival of religion? This question has remained a subject of discussion for a long period of time. In my view, an answer can be found, which, while accepting the full importance of Tabligh work, also acknowledges the need to provide intellectual satisfaction to those who want to work in other fields as well, provided that on an intellectual plane they are able to relate the different aspects of the work as a whole, thus serving the same purpose from different angles.

My study of the Quran and the Hadith has brought me to the conclusion that the demands of religion are of two kinds. The first is related to the essence, the soul of religion; the realization of God, the establishment of a relationship of fear and hope, of trust, of submission to Him in all one's affairs, be they spiritual or material.

The second demand is temporal, created by circumstances. It is true that religion does at times come into conflict with other ideologies in the world. It is challenged at various points, and to defend it and maintain its intellectual and material status, we have to deal with a great diversity of situations in different ways. Sometimes it becomes urgent to make peace, as at Hudaibiyya, and sometimes defence is urgently called for, as at Badr and Hunain. At other times we have to take recourse to rational arguments when religion comes face to face with such thoughts as subvert its very basis, as has happened in the past when Muslims were exposed to Greek thought.

The former demand concerns the essence of religion and is permanently to be desired; the latter is a relative part of religion determined by the circumstances. At times the relative part assumes the same importance as the real; but when the need vanishes it loses its importance.

If this interpretation is acceptable, I think we can relate all parts to a cohesive whole, bringing together all of them on one platform in order to work for the same cause. Thus all of us can share in the revival of religion according to our capacities. What we all desire, but have failed to achieve, is to create a united platform. Due emphasis must be accorded to the Tabligh work and the important part played by it in reviving the essence of religion. This is my view as regards the main mission of Tabligh, but not as regards the particular method of working that they have adopted, since the method of functioning of any movement or party is purely relative.

While the importance of the Tabligh mission must be accepted, the need to work in different arenas is also acute. Capable people from the Ummah should come forward to share in this gigantic task of Islamic revival. If they are sincere in its pursuit, the Tabligh people must give them due recognition and encouragement. They should even help them at an individual level.

In the latter half of the 20th century some of the issues facing us are: the restoration of the honour and dominance of the Muslims in the modern world, the compilation of Islamic law according to the needs of modern times, the preparation of a new system of education for Muslims which caters to present needs and situations, the preparation of missionary literature, keeping in view the requirements of the modern mind and challenges from modern ideologies. All these objectives call for a defence of religion on an academic level. It is beyond a single person or a group to perform all these tasks. What is desirable is that the importance of one another's work be recognized. There should be mutual consultation and assistance. The coordination that is required can be illustrated by the example of the electricity which is generated in the power house and the machines which are produced in factories. Their utility would be zero if they did not meet at some point. It is by their relating to one another that they acquire meaning and efficacy. If such unity is achieved on an intellectual level by the Ummah, it will eventually bring immense benefits. The revival of Islam which, for centuries had been an empty dream, will become a reality in a matter of years or even just months.